Herbert Baxter Adams

**Notes on the Literature of Charities**

Herbert Baxter Adams

**Notes on the Literature of Charities**

ISBN/EAN: 9783337205515

Printed in Europe, USA, Canada, Australia, Japan

Cover: Foto ©Thomas Meinert / pixelio.de

More available books at **www.hansebooks.com**

# VIII

## NOTES

ON THE

# LITERATURE OF CHARITIES

JOHNS HOPKINS UNIVERSITY STUDIES

IN

HISTORICAL AND POLITICAL SCIENCE

HERBERT B. ADAMS, Editor

---

History is past Politics and Politics present History — *Freeman*

---

FIFTH SERIES

VIII

# NOTES

ON THE

# LITERATURE OF CHARITIES

BY HERBERT B. ADAMS

---

BALTIMORE

PUBLICATION AGENCY OF THE JOHNS HOPKINS UNIVERSITY

AUGUST, 1887

JOHN MURPHY & CO., PRINTERS,
BALTIMORE.

# CONTENTS.

# NOTES

# LITERATURE OF CHARITIES.[1]

A recent discussion in Baltimore of the subject of organized charities has quickened popular interest in the subject and has stimulated further inquiry. Public spirited citizens and university students are beginning to seek more systematic and detailed information respecting the history and operation of organized charitable effort. Literature here comes to our aid. It can supply a perpetual fountain of knowledge, experience, and enthusiasm for practical work.

## BALTIMORE.

For Baltimore readers the literature of charities, like charity itself, begins at home. Our first duty is to inquire for local

---

[1] This paper was prepared for a popular audience and a local purpose. It was read, in selected parts, at the closing meeting of the Conference on Charities held in Baltimore, April 15–16, 1887, and is now published in a revised form to meet a public need. Without attempting bibliographical completeness, the writer has aimed to present a suggestive description of some of the best and most available literature on charities. For valuable references and occasional comments, acknowledgment is due to President D. C. Gilman, Dr. Richard T. Ely, Dr. J. F. Jameson, Dr. Edward W. Bemis, Professor G. Stanley Hall, Dr. Fabian Franklin, Messrs. Gardner, Warner, Young, and Tuska, of the Johns Hopkins University. Use has been made of some of the best known catalogues and of the Co-operative Index. The writer has merely endeavored to give unity and point to a great variety of scattered materials.

7

contributions to the subject.   Perhaps the best work to begin
with is the Rev. William F. Slocum, Jr.'s excellent tract on
the Relation of Private and Public to Organized Charity,
recently published by the Charity Organization of this city.
The work is written in vigorous English and tells some plain
but startling facts.   For example, twenty persons receiving
charity from one church in Baltimore were found by inquiry
to be all impostors.   The reasons and necessity for co-operation
in charitable work are clearly set forth, and the best experience
of this country and Europe is cited.   Dr. Richard T. Ely's
admirable paper on the general principles of philanthropy,
with respect to charities, should be read by every student.
The article was originally published in the Baltimore Sun,
March 9, 1887, but it has recently been republished by the
Charity Organization Society and deserves renewed attention.
Other important articles upon charity organization in Baltimore have appeared from time to time in the Baltimore
papers.  .There are readable articles on the Organization of
Charity in *The Sun* for March 15, 1887, and in *The Daily
News,* for March 26, 1887.   *The Sun* showed that the total
number of applications for relief during the four months pre-
ceding March, 1887, was 2,003, and the number of investiga-
tions was 1,161.   During the time 199 vagrants were dealt
with, 149 frauds were exposed or suppressed, and 138 street
beggars were warned.   Of the whole number, 209 persons were
found to need not relief but work, and employment was
secured by the society for 152.   256 cases were put on record
as undeserving, and 200 false addresses were found out.   The
society placed 101 of the applicants in institutions appropriate
to their needs.   Assistance was obtained for 618 (in 378 cases,
from other societies and in 240, from individuals).   Seven
loans were made, which, as a rule, have had good results.
102 of the cases were dismissed because they had become self-
sustaining.   The agents of the society made 2,158 official
visits, besides the large number of calls made by the various
friendly visitors of the district board.

## PHILADELPHIA.

After an examination of the home-field, it will be found profitable to turn to the experience of our neighbors. Philadelphia has been at work for several years in organizing local charities. The annual reports of the central board of directors to the society for organizing charity are full of interesting suggestions. "What shall Philadelphia do with its Paupers?" was the subject of a paper by Dr. Isaac Ray, published in the *Penn Monthly* in April, 1873, and republished by the Philadelphia Social Science Association, whose proceedings contain many other valuable papers. For example, among those read at the ninth annual meeting was an article by the Rev. William H. Hodge on "The Philadelphia Society for organizing Charitable Relief and repressing Mendicancy." The same general subject is treated in the *Penn Monthly* for September, 1878. Excellent "Suggestions to Ward-Visitors" have been given in published form by Mrs. Susan I. Lesley, of Philadelphia. The Rev. D. O. Kellogg contributed an article on the organization of Charity in Philadelphia, to the *Penn Monthly* for September, 1878. The Pauper Question by the same author was published in the *Atlantic Monthly* for May, 1883, and was republished by the Charity Organization of New York. The annual reports of the Public Charities of Pennsylvania are a trustworthy source of information. The annual reports of the directors of City Trusts in Philadelphia are also standard.

## NEW YORK.

The experience of New York, in matters pertaining to charity, has been extensive and valuable. Interesting experiments in social reform have been tried in the metropolis and in New York state institutions. A general view of the whole subject is presented in Prof. Theodore W. Dwight's paper in the Journal of American Social Science, No. 2, on the Public Charities of the State of New York. The annual reports of the State Board of Charities and the reports of the State Charities Aid Association are standard. In the former series, tenth report, appeared Dr. Charles S. Hoyt's paper on the Causes of Pauperism, afterward republished as a pamphlet. In the latter series was printed Miss Schuyler's article on the Importance of uniting Individual and Associated Volunteer Effort in Behalf of the Poor, also issued as a pamphlet. A useful Handbook for Friendly Visitors among the Poor was published by the Putnams for the Charity Organization Society of New York City. The Putnams have also published, in their " Questions of the Day," Mrs. Josephine Shaw Lowell's excellent article on Public Relief and Private Charity.' This is one of the most concise and available authorities. It urges organization of charities, the promotion of self-help, with industrial and moral training. Mrs. Lowell is the author of a valuable report on vagrancy, presented at a meeting of the New York State Board of Charities. A paper on Charitable Organization and Administration, by the Rev. Henry C. Potter, D. D., was read before an Episcopal Church congress and published in New York in 1877.

Excellent work has been done by the Board of Relief of the United Hebrew Charities of New York City. The 12th report, published in 1886, shows that of 2,805 applications for employment, 1,600 secured good places, 146 as clerks, 713 as operatives, 198 as office boys, 120 as porters, 102 as salesmen, 111 as waiters and nurses, 68 as book-keepers, 59 as drivers, 11 as teachers, etc. This is a remarkable contribution to self-help in one city by one system of charities. Hebrew charities have been well described by Miss Mary H. Cohen in the Journal of American Social Science, No. 19. The Catholic Charities of New York are treated by L. B. Binsse, in the Catholic World, 43: 681, 809.

Helen Campbell has made valuable contributions to the literature of charities (1) in her study of the problem of the poor, a Record of Quiet Work in Unquiet Places, New York, 1882, and (2) in her book on Prisoners of Poverty, recently published by the Roberts Brothers of Boston, 1887. This work is a collection of newspaper articles which originally appeared in the New York *Tribune* and which throw strong light on the economic slavery which exists in the great metropolis.

Very interesting and remarkable are the writings of Mr. Charles Loring Brace: (1) the Dangerous Classes of New York, and Twenty Years Work among them; (2) the Care of Poor and Vicious Children, Journal of the American Social Science Association, No. 11; (3) in the same Journal, No. 18, Child Helping in New York; (4) the annual reports of the Children's Aid Society. Baltimoreans who remember Mr. Brace's account of this work at the recent Charity Conference will read these papers with deep interest. An extraordinary study into the effects of crime, pauperism, disease, and heredity is that called " The Jukes," by Richard L. Dugdale, New York, 1877, published by G. P. Putnam's Sons.

The Problem of Pauperism in Brooklyn has been considered in a pamphlet by the Hon. Seth Low. This apostle of municipal reform has also treated the subject of Out-Door Relief in the United States, in a report read at a National Conference of Charities and Corrections and reprinted as a pamphlet.

One of the most helpful of all works upon the subject of Charity Organization is that written by the Rev. S. H. Gurteen, of Buffalo, N. Y. The book represents wide reading and observation. It is both historical and practical. Mr. Gurteen is also the author of a good paper entitled " What is Charity Organization?" Buffalo, 1881.

## New England.

Here lies another rich field of organized charities which may be studied by means of literature. Mr. F. B. Sanborn's report on the public charities of Massachusetts, prepared for the centennial commission in 1876, presents an excellent history of the origin and development of all the charities of a typical

New England Commonwealth. The annual reports of the State Board of Health, Lunacy, and Charity are invaluable. Mr. F. B. Sanborn has treated the subject of Poor-Law Administration in New England in the *North American Review*, 114 : 1. The same writer has a paper in the transactions of the American Social Science Association, No. 1, June, 1869, on the Supervision of Charities.

The Charities of Boston are described by Mr. Samuel A. Eliot in the *North American Review*, 61 : 135 (1845). The new movement in charitable work receives special attention from H. A. Stimson and D. McGregor Means in the *Andover Review*, 3 : 107 and 4 : 220. Charity Organization is treated in the *New Englander and Yale Review* for March, 1887. The annual reports of the Associated Charities of Boston will be found instructive. In 1886 was published a directory of all the benevolent and charitable organizations in that city. This work is a model of its kind and a *vade mecum* for the practical worker. Its bibliography of charity has been of service to the writer in supplementing the present sketch. The book not only describes all the existing agencies in Boston for distributing charity, but it contains also a useful summary of Massachusetts legislation touching charities, health, the liquor traffic, etc. Similar directories have been published in New York and Baltimore, but good suggestions for a new edition may be derived from the Boston directory which is the latest of all. The original idea of these directories came from London, which still has a model guide of charity.

Many contributions to the administration of charity have been published in Boston, notably Mrs. James T. Fields' How to Help the Poor; Joseph Tuckerman's work on The Elevation of the Poor, with an introduction by Rev. Dr. E. E. Hale. One of the earliest contributions was a translation by Mrs. Horace Mann and Miss Peabody, in 1832, of Joseph Marie de Gérando's *Le Visiteur du Pauvre*, published in Boston as The Visitor of the Poor. The report of a Boston commission on the Treatment of the Poor was issued in 1878.

The annual reports of the Industrial Aid Society should be consulted.

Other states and cities in this country besides those mentioned have published valuable reports of their systems of charity. The Boston Directory shows that charity organization societies now exist in more than fifty different municipal centres and in twenty different states. The extension of the system will rapidly increase the literature of organized charities. It is highly desirable that a good reference-library of special reports, pamphlets, monographs, and newspaper comment should be collected in every new centre of organization. This class of literature is necessarily ephemeral, and it can never become accessible to the public unless it is gathered and systematically arranged by the local agents of organized charity. When valuable reports or published addresses appear, these agents should review them for the daily press, so that thousands may read the results of one man's study.

## American Periodicals.

There are several periodicals which should be familiar to all charity-workers. First, that called *Lend a Hand*, edited by the Rev. Edward Everett Hale. This magazine is readable and popular in the best sense. In every number are suggestive stories and brief summaries of the reports of many charitable societies. The editorials discuss such subjects as the difference between pauperism and poverty, and the principles of charity organization. An article which appeared in the first number of *Lend a Hand*, describing the abuses which prevailed in a prison belonging to the United States, led to an examination and remedy of those abuses by authority of Congress. Among other interesting information afforded by this magazine is an account of the attempts made in this country to introduce co-operative manufactures.

*The Monthly Register*, published in Philadelphia, is the official organ of twenty societies of Organized Charity. The

Bulletin of the New York Charity Organization Society is published monthly and is concerned chiefly with the local work in that city, but it is full of suggestions for workers elsewhere.  *The Friend* is a New York journal of charity, published at 150 Nassau Street.

*The International Record of Charities and Correction,* edited by F. H. Wines, has just begun its second volume.  It is a very valuable repertory of all that pertains to the administration of prisons, reformatories, houses of correction, juvenile asylums, and other forms of state or local organization for the prevention of poverty and crime.

The publications of the American Economic Association are likely to prove of great practical value to the friends of the poor and of the working classes.  Most valuable is the series of papers upon the subject of Co-operation in the United States : (1) Co-operation in a Western City, by Albert Shaw, Ph. D., now one of the editors of the Minneapolis Tribune. (2) Co-operation in New England, by E. W. Bemis, Ph. D. (3) Three phases of Co-operation in the West, by A. G. Warner, former Fellow in History, of the Johns Hopkins University, now general agent of the Charity Organization Society in Baltimore.  These papers, with others upon the same class of subjects, are written by Baltimore university men, and are soon to be collected and published in book-form in the " Johns Hopkins University Studies in Historical and Political Science."

The publications of the American Social Science Association and of the Social Science Association of Philadelphia are rich in contributions to subjects pertaining to the improvement of society.  A file of the proceedings of these two Associations is most desirable for every bureau of organized charities.  Among the papers of the society first named, in addition to others already mentioned, are: Associated Charities (No. 12); American Factory Life, by Miss Lucy Larcom (No. 16); Tenement Houses, by Dr. L. M. Hall (No. 20).

The proceedings of the Annual Conferences of Charities

and Corrections are among the fullest of all American sources
of information respecting the charitable work actually accomplished in this country and the methods employed in the different states and cities. These reports of conferences serve as
a kind of national repository for all local experience in the
organization and promotion of charities. Interesting reformatory and sociological experiments are also recorded here.

## ORGANIZED CHARITIES IN ENGLAND.

The best original sources of information are the reports and
publications of the London Charity Organization Society and
the Charity Organization Review, published monthly. The
latter is full of substantial, detailed information, stated in a
practical business-like way. If one wishes to descend from the
contemplative heights of principle, from sentimental or purely
scientific interest in the subject of charities, to practical every
day work, this organ of actual experience in London districts
will tell what to do and how to do it. The London Journal
and official reports are received by the Charity Organization
Society of Baltimore and may be seen at their office.

*The Hospital* is an English Journal, published by an
association and designed to give the latest information upon
hospital work and kindred charities.

Various works of a suggestive character have been published
in England upon the best methods of charitable work, *e. g.*,
A Handy Book for Visitors of the Poor in London, by Charles
B. P. Bosanquet, secretary of the Charity Organization Society
of London; Sir Charles Trevelyan on Systematic Visitation
of the Poor in their own Homes; Thoughts and Experiences
of a Charity Organizationist, by J. N. Hornsby Wright;
Method in Almsgiving, by M. W. Moggridge; Suggestions
to the Charitable for Systematic Inquiry into the Cases of
Applicants for Relief, by C. J. Ribton-Turner; Report of the
Local Government Board, for 1873–4, with papers by Octavia
Hill and others, upon subjects relating to charity.

Ginx's Baby, a satire, is a healthful warning against red-tape methods of exercising charity. A baby, born in a London slum and abandoned by its parents, is tossed about and quarrelled over by various officials and charitable associations of London. The book is out of print, but by no means out of date.

English Charity Organization is the subject of a valuable article recently published in the Baltimore *Sun*, March 30, 1887. The article was written by Mr. D. R. Randall, of Annapolis, fellow in history at the Johns Hopkins University, with some valuable additions by Mr. John Glenn. It is based upon material like that already cited and upon Judge Fisher's inquiries in England. The essay is reprinted as an appendix to this sketch of the literature of charities as a local contribution to the subject, and as a good illustration of how special knowledge, study, and observation may be popularized and made useful through the daily press. It is interesting for example, to read, in the above sketch, of the work of Thomas Chalmers in Glasgow and of Octavia Hill who is called " the centre of a planetary system of workers who have the care of three thousand tenants in the city of London." This latter work is of special interest to Baltimoreans because it is founded upon the model tenement-house system, established for the poor of London by George Peabody.

### Thomas Arnold.

One of the earliest of modern Englishmen to interest himself in the moral elevation of the masses and in the proper application of charity was Thomas Arnold, the head-master of Rugby. The reading of his biography, written by the late Dean Stanley, will afford a good starting-point for the study of that interesting movement called Christian socialism, which is now spreading over England. This movement means the organized and personal effort of good Christians to regenerate the lower strata of English society. Dr. Arnold's essay on

"The Social Condition of the Operative Classes," reprinted in the volume called Arnold's Miscellaneous Works, from his original letters to the Sheffield *Courant*, in 1832, is highly suggestive. The essay teaches the great historian's practical method of utilizing the daily press for reformatory work. Arnold even founded and supported for a time a newspaper of his own, conducted in the interest of social reform. He maintained that society "should put the poor man, being a freeman, into a situation where he may live as a freeman ought to live." In Arnold's view the great agencies for the social reform of England are the Christian Church and the English aristocracy. In a letter to Mr. Justice Coleridge, Dr. Arnold said, "I would give anything to be able to organize a Society 'for drawing public attention to the state of the laboring classes throughout the kingdom.' . . . A Society might give the alarm, and present the facts to the notice of the public. It was thus that Clarkson overthrew the slave trade."

## English Biography.

Following Arnold came the social reformers, Frederick Denison Maurice, Charles Kingsley, Thomas Hughes, and Frederick W. Robertson. If one would realize from concrete examples how useful a single human life may be in the improvement of the condition of society, he should study the work of these men. The life of Maurice, chiefly as told in his own letters, has been edited by his son, Colonel Frederick Maurice, in two interesting volumes. A good *résumé* of the same may be found in the *Contemporary Review* for March, 1884. Letters and Memories of the life of Charles Kingsley, by his wife, have also been given to the public. Thomas Hughes' life-work is known and read of all men who are interested in the progress of practical Christianity in England. The Life, Letters, Lectures, and Addresses of Robertson have been edited by Stopford A. Brooke and published by the Harpers in New York. A series of lectures upon these christian workers has been given by Baltimore clergymen and others to university men on Sunday afternoons and should be repeated to workingmen.

Symington's biographical sketch of Thomas Chalmers, who very early engaged in the reformation of charities in Glasgow, should be studied. There is a good article upon Chalmers in the Encyclopædia Britannica. The writings of Chalmers upon Charities are very important, notably his treatment of the Parochial System and Pauperism, and the Civic Economy of large Towns. The autobiography and memoir of Thomas Guthrie are also to be recommended. To the biographical literature of charities belong the Letters and other Writings of Edward Denison, M. P., for Newark, and the Life and Letters of James Hinton.

Among recent biographies, the Life of Lord Shaftsbury deserves the first place, because of the excellence of the character displayed, the long and eventful period which the memoir covers, and the great variety of social problems to which reference is made. The three volumes are too extended for general perusal, but they will be found most serviceable for reference particularly as to the employment and proper care of neglected children, the housing of the poor, the supervision of lodging-houses, the improvement of insane asylums, and the promotion of temperance. Legislation in respect to factory operatives is another of the themes to which Lord Shaftsbury devoted a great deal of thought. It would be difficult to name any work which gives a more comprehensive review of the charitable movements in London during the reign of Queen Victoria.

The Life of James Fraser, Bishop of Manchester, recently written by Thomas Hughes, illustrates the efficiency of an Oxford Fellow, called from a country parish to be the head of a diocese in which all the modern industrial problems are being worked out on a grand scale. He devoted himself without reserve to the promotion of all good things in Lancashire and was sometimes called the Bishop of the Laity and sometimes the Bishop of the Dissenters, so ready was he to co-operate with all Christian workers. The education of the people was one of the subjects in which he was most interested and to many people in this country he is chiefly known for his report upon American Schools; but the Labor Question, and the subordinate matters of Trades Unions and Co-operation, exercised his mind during all his episcopate. He was a noble man, as exemplary and as inspiring as any one who has lived in England since Maurice and Kingsley.

Passing from the lives of men, eminent for their work in social reform, let us note the Lives of Miss Carpenter of Bristol, of Sister Dora, and of Elizabeth Fry as among those which are helpful to all who are interested in the work of women, in the improvement of prisons, hospitals, and reformatories. The useful lives and writings of Octavia and Florence Hill, who have done much for improving the housing of the poor, cannot be studied too carefully.

### ARNOLD TOYNBEE.

One of the most interesting modern developments of enlightened charity and Christian socialism in England is the Oxford University movement in the great city of London. A few years ago Arnold Toynbee, tutor of Balliol College, Oxford, and a company of his friends, graduates of that institution, took hold of the almost hopeless task of reforming East London. "For several months in successive years," says Professor Jowett, the biographer of Toynbee, "he resided in Whitechapel, and undertook the duties of a visitor for the Charity Organization Society. There he lived in half-furnished lodgings, as far as he could after the manner of working men, joining in their clubs, discussing with them (sometimes in an atmosphere of bad whiskey, bad tobacco, bad drainage) things material and spiritual—the laws of Nature and of God." Toynbee set himself resolutely against some of the extreme socialistic views of men who had been excited by agitators and misled by theorists.   Indeed, he lost his life (1882), at the early age of thirty, in combating economic error upon the lecturer's platform.   He was, however, no champion of the " dismal science."   He was one of the most gifted apostles of the New Political Economy[1] which means humanity in business and everyday life.   Toynbee understood affairs, both high and low.   He was the treasurer of Balliol College, Oxford, and the true friend of the workingman.   If you would know what he thought about Political Economy, read his published lectures on the Industrial Revolution in England, together with a short memoir of the author by Professor Jowett, master of Balliol College (Rivingtons, London, 1884). If you would know what people are beginning to think about Toynbee and his work, read the short sketch of " Toynbee Hall," in the May number (1887) of *The Century.*

Although the young economist died, his friends took up his social mission and established a colony of Oxford graduates in East London, the workingmen's quarter.   Money was raised; Toynbee Hall was erected.   There these students live and work.   The building is the headquarters of the organized charities of East London; it contains a lecture-hall, where popular instruction and good concerts are given.   Classes in history and political economy, reading clubs, singing classes, drawing classes, magic lantern illustrations of geography, instruction for the deaf and dumb, training in the practical arts,—all these things and many more have been instituted at Toynbee Hall in the notorious East End.   In *Lend a Hand,* May, 1887, there is an article upon Toynbee's work, by the Rev. J. S. Gilman, showing that between twenty and thirty university men were engaged last year in charitable work in connection with Toynbee Hall.   Expenses were met by grad-

---

[1] The change which is coming over English economic thought is most decided at the Universities of Oxford and Cambridge.   It is well represented by the article on " Political Economy," by J. K. Ingram, of Trinity College, Dublin, in the new edition of the Encyclopædia Britannica.

uates and undergraduates of Oxford and other universities. Indeed, the whole work of Toynbee Hall is sometimes spoken of as "The Universities' Settlement in East London."

It is worthy of note that these young Englishmen do not affect any appearance of roughness in their dress and manner, nor any austerity in their mode of life. Toynbee Hall is really an English University Club established in East London. University-men have comfortable, well-furnished rooms, with private libraries and all the conveniences of student-life that are possible in a university colony. To affect asceticism and poverty would be to repeat the mistake of mediæval monks. The idea of the men of Toynbee Hall is to carry university-culture into the very heart of East London in social, civilizing, reforming ways. Workingmen do not think any the less of these manly, athletic young fellows because they live like gentlemen. On the contrary, East London people are proud of having university men as neighbors and would perhaps send them all to Parliament, to represent the labor party, if that were possible by an East-End *plébiscite*. Toynbee Hall has all the advantages of a modern English Club and all the virtues of a Benedictine monastery. It is a centre of learning and civilization in a savage district. It is a shining example of well-ordered, social life. Every workingmen's club in the East End will sooner or later be improved and elevated by the influence of Toynbee Hall.

It is an interesting and suggestive fact that a work similar to the social mission of Oxford students in London has been for some time in progress in the poorer quarters of the city of New York. A few college graduates, some from Amherst, men studying theology or practising law, and two or three young instructors connected with Columbia College, are carrying the germs of moral and social reform into the very worst regions of the metropolis. At least one College-man has taken comfortable lodgings in lower New York and often invites a few poor people to his cheerful rooms for a pleasant evening to meet his student friends. This healthy, hearty spirit of good-fellowship and social endeavor, without cant and sham, is the result of various influences, ethical, religious, and personal.   Not the least is that of Mr. Stanton Coit and other Amherst men.   Some idea of what sort of moral leaven is working among some of the college and university men of New York City, and elsewhere, may be had from an article on the Christian Socialists, in the *Political Science Quarterly* for June, 1886, by Dr. Edwin R. A. Seligman.   It is a most appreciative sketch of the life-work of Frederick Denison Maurice, Charles Kingsley, and of the modern English movement toward the application of Christian ethics to actual life. Christian realism or secularized Christianity is by no means confined to England.   It pervades France and Germany.   It crops out in Russia in Tolstoi, the Russian novelist, who lives and works among his peasants.   It is the old spirit in new and practical forms.

### SOCIOLOGICAL NOVELS.

Toynbee Hall is the headquarters of the " Beaumont Trust " which is the economic basis of the People's Palace, opened by the Queen May 14, 1887, but foreshadowed by Charles Kingsley's " Alton Locke " and Walter Besant's " All Sorts and Conditions of Men."   (Besant describes the People's Palace in the *Contemporary Review* for February, 1887.)   These novels, together with Besant's " Children of Gibeon," throw a flood of light upon the actual condition of the working classes of England, their mode of life, their natural attitude toward their own elevation, toward capital, and the higher organizations of society, whether school, college, church, or state.   Invaluable suggestions are given to well-disposed persons, showing them how they may succeed in giving practical shape to their philanthropic efforts, so as to avoid disappointment and waste of energy.   Sociological novels like these, and George Eliot's " Felix Holt," and Miss Fothergill's Lancashire stories, have already accomplished great good in England.   That country, in spite of its landlordism and class-distinctions, is many years nearer the enlightenment of human selfishness, nearer the ultimate harmony of capital and labor, nearer the economic organization of Christian charity, nearer self-help and honest government than is our own country.  The way to an appreciation of these facts lies through English social science and a study of the work actually in progress in English manufacturing districts, where workingmen in many instances, through successful organization, have become small capitalists and whence they send to Parliament, instead of ignorant demagogues, men of intelligence and property, who are really the best friends of the common people.  The time is surely coming in America, if it is not already here, when workingmen will recognize that there are other forms of labor than the work of men's hands; that their own brain and skill and economic thrift are forms of capital.  Indeed the *labor of capital* and the *capital of labor* will some day become convertible terms.

## WORKINGMEN'S CLUBS.

An article in the *Christian Union* for May 5, 1887, shows that, at the present time, there are in London about one hundred workingmen's clubs, or voluntary, self-supporting labor associations.  They are most numerous in East London and their membership varies from 250 to 1,000.  They have their own halls of assembly, often a billiard-room or restaurant. Frequently the clubs have reading-rooms and lecture-halls. Lectures are usually given on Sunday.  The opinions of the laboring classes are moulded in these clubs.  Here are the centres of agitation upon economic and political questions. These clubs are often the scenes of noisy discussion and of socialistic argumentation : but the English workingman is usually a very sensible fellow, far more likely to be moved by practical considerations than by mere theories of the reconstruction of society.  Walter Besant says, in his article on the Amusements of the People, (*Contem. Rev.*, March, 1884) " our English workingman is not a firebrand, and though he listens

to an immense quantity of fiery oratory, and reads endless
fiery articles, he has the good sense to perceive that none of
the destructive measures recommended by his friends are
likely to improve his own wages or reduce the price of food."
In very many instances, as in our own country, the workingman's instinct and judgment upon public questions are very
sound.

A valuable article on the Political Education of Workingmen appeared in the Boston *Advertiser*, October 27, 1882,
describing the work of the Social and Political Education
League, of which Professor J. R. Seeley, of Cambridge, is
president, and of which London is the centre. The work
consists of lectures by educated men upon questions of the
day. The lectures are given in the workingmen's halls and
clubs, wherever an opportunity is afforded. The necessary
expenses, cost of advertising, etc., are met by the local organization. Such subjects are treated as Cavour and Modern
Italy, Bismarck and Socialism, the Constitution of the United
States, the Participation of Labor in the Profits of Capital,
etc. The work of this Education League is not partisan. It
is the idea of Professor Seeley that the English people, like
university students, can be taught to study politics and social
problems in a scientific, unprejudiced way. "He has com-
pletely renovated historical studies in his own university of
Cambridge, and he is of the opinion that the same kind of
work which has been carried on amongst university students
might, on a more limited scale, be undertaken amongst the
more intelligent workingmen." Some of the leading pro-
fessors of England, James Bryce, Bonamy Price, and A. V.
Dicey, have taken a part in this useful work.

There is also in England, among the workingmen, a great
deal of political education along party-lines. For several
years, the liberal party has been vigorously engaged in the
propaganda of liberal doctrines among the workingmen by
means of popular lectures. The machinery of workingmen's
clubs is everywhere employed. The great centres of activity
are London, Birmingham, and Manchester.

A most interesting development among the common people is the parliamentary debating society, for the discussion of public questions. It is based upon the forms of procedure now in vogue in the house of commons. The societies have their speaker and sergeant-at-arms; the mace plays its ancient part in preserving order; there is a ministerial party and an opposition; bills are introduced and debated with all'due formality. These miniature parliaments are awakening political intelligence throughout all England. As a means of education they are quite as valuable as New England town-meetings. England is re-creating herself politically by this popular exercise of free speech and the forms of self-government.

## UNIVERSITY-EXTENSION LECTURES.

An instructive account of the remarkable sociological experiment now in progress in the manufacturing district of Manchester was lately given by one of its representatives, Mr. Rowley, to the students of history and political science at the Johns Hopkins University and was reported in the Baltimore papers (*Sun* and *American*) for April 6, 1887. Mr. Rowley described the successful co-operative efforts of the workingmen and their friends to make life more tolerable among the cinder heaps of that great manufacturing city. He told us of the system of "University-Extension" lectures which are given under the auspices of a workingmen's association or labor institute. This system of education is not superimposed upon the men, but they themselves, under good leadership, have organized it and pay for it, at least in part. The workingmen, through their secretary, send up to the University of Oxford asking for a lecturer on English history or Political Economy.[1] The University Senate appoints the

---

[1] A text-book on "The Economics of Industry" by Alfred and Mary Marshall "was undertaken at the request of a meeting of Cambridge University-Extension lecturers" and was published by Macmillan, 1885.

man, usually an enterprising tutor, of the Toynbee school, who is abreast with the times and in sympathy with his fellow men. He goes to Manchester for a small fee and his expenses. Not only are interesting lecture-courses given to appreciative audiences, but class-courses and examinations have been instituted. Public readings are also given. Excellent concerts are afforded. Choice literature is distributed in inexpensive editions. The managers insist upon having the best, whether in reading, music, or lectures. Second rate performances are ruled out and professional bores are not tolerated. The most encouraging thing about this experiment is that it promotes organized self-help and partly pays for itself. Similar experiments have been undertaken in other parts of England. An interesting description of "The Extension of University Teaching" not only by Oxford but by Cambridge, Owens College, the Victoria University, etc., may be found in *The American* (Philadelphia), April 30, 1887. The writer, John Leyland, says the scheme is under contemplation by the universities of Scotland and has already been adopted by the University of Sydney, Australia. A pamphlet on the University-Extension Movement, by Richard G. Moulton, M. A., Cambridge, with an introduction by Professor Stuart, M. P., has been published by Bemrose and Sons, 23 Old Bailey, London, Price 3d. The pamphlet contains all the business-details connected with this novel system of carrying higher education from university centres to the people at large. Professor Stuart says "It embodies the experience of the Cambridge University-Extension Movement, in connection with which six hundred courses of lectures and classes have been held during the last ten years, with a total of sixty thousand pupils of nearly all classes of society, and in most districts of England." The system aims at popular audiences, in which a nucleus of earnest students, men and women, is always found. Arrangements are made by local committees. The University simply supplies lecturers. It should be remembered by all passive admirers of this interesting educational experiment that it has its business-side. It is a question of local demand and central supply. Education, like all true charity, should be so directed as to yield, if possible, some economic return. Moral returns, the promotion of intelligence and individual energy, go without saying. Any system of educational philanthrophy which gives everything and exacts nothing is in danger of becoming prodigal waste. It is not to be expected that the higher education can ever be made to pay in dollars and cents, but it should not be demanded by the people as a free gift. Even common schools are supported by taxing the community which they profit. In England it has been found by experience that fully one-half of the expense of University-extension lectures can be met by the sale of tickets; the balance is obtained by subscription and private philanthropy. In a large sense, the outlay pays; it results in the moral, social, and intellectual elevation of great towns and manufacturing districts. The small fees paid by workingmen for their own improvement are an investment of untold value, yielding returns not only in useful knowledge but in character and manly independence which are beyond price.

## AMUSEMENTS FOR THE PEOPLE.

Charity often takes other forms than the giving of food and raiment. Popular amusements of an elevating kind, such as public readings, lectures, concerts, free days in museums and galleries of art, the use of circulating libraries, book and magazine clubs, recreation grounds, open air sports, entertainments in summer, good music, winter gardens, are eminently worthy of charitable and organized effort. One of the most suggestive and valuable books in this line is Washington Gladden's Applied Christianity (see also his article in *The Century*, January, 1885, on Christianity and Popular Amusements). The gospel of green grass and fresh air needs to be presented now and then to the working people. Most sensible

arc the words of Octavia Hill in her charming essay on Open
Spaces (see her book on Our Common Land). She advocates
" the provision of small open spaces, planted and made pretty,
quite near the homes of the people, which might be used by
them in common as sitting-rooms in summer." She says
" There are two great wants in the life of the poor in our
large towns, which ought to be realised more than they are—
the want of space, and the want of beauty." These wants are
even more conspicuous in some of our American cities than
in Old England, where, in proportion to the population,
vastly more open space is preserved in public squares than
with us.

It is, however, deserving of note that in certain manufacturing districts of this country, employers have shown a humane
regard for the health, comfort, and recreation of their employees. South Manchester, Connecticut, has been made a Para-
dise of labor by the Cheney Brothers, although upon the
paternal plan, resembling the experiment at Pullman, Illinois.
At South Manchester there are model tenement houses, with
gardens attached, for the cultivation of flowers and vegeta-
bles. The town has gas, water, concrete walks, and plenty of
green grass. Games, lectures, amateur theatricals, etc., are
encouraged by the proprietors. In Harper's Magazine for
November, 1872, there is an illustrated article by Edward
Howland on the Industrial Experiment at South Manchester.
Dr. Richard T. Ely, in Harper's Magazine for February,
1885, has given a less favorable view of Pullman.[1] At Ashton,

---

[1] An earlier industrial experiment than Pullman or South Manchester
was that at Saltaire, a model manufacturing town, founded in 1853 by Sir
Titus Salt upon the river Aire in Yorkshire, England. This town has a
social club or literary institute, with a cheerful library, class rooms, a
gymnasium, billiard room, and a large hall for lectures, readings, concerts,
etc. Fees for membership are very low so that the privileges of the institute are brought within the reach of all. One half of the board of governors
of this social club are appointed by the capitalists and the other half are
elected by the operatives. A beautiful park of fourteen acres was laid out

Rhode Island, the Lonsdale Company, which owns various mills along the Blackstone river, purchased some time ago recreation grounds opposite their mills for the encouragement of open-air games among their workingmen.

The Rev. Robert Murray, Jr., writing of this experiment to Mr. W. E. Foster, of Providence, says: "The Lonsdale Company has always pursued a liberal and thoughtful policy towards their employees, and it seemed to them that it would be an excellent thing for them to have such grounds, to which they could resort on the Saturday half holidays, and on the long summer evenings." Mr. Murray says that, when the grounds were first opened, addresses were made by the superintendent, by a Catholic priest and by an Episcopal clergyman. "These grounds consist, I should say, of forty or fifty acres. They are on a sort of plateau that rises eighty or one hundred feet above the Blackstone river. They are fringed by a young growth of trees, which in a few years will be large enough to furnish a grateful shade. The approach to them along the river banks and through quite a stretch of woodland is very pleasant. They are duly appreciated by the operatives, and they resort to them every pleasant Saturday afternoon to witness or take part in games of cricket, base ball, or foot ball; and they have occasional picnics on the ground, at which they remain on moonlit nights till ten o'clock or later. I think they answer an excellent purpose and have met a great need

---

along the bank of the river Aire in 1871. The river-site is convenient for boating and for bathing-places. Saltaire has its factory-schools, its churches. infirmaries, and other model institutions. Although the town was created by the mill-owners, the purchase of land-lots and the erection of cottages by operatives is encouraged. "Sir Titus has taught the English capitalist to what noble duties it is possible to devote himself, and the English laborer that the barrier between the sympathies of the master that overlooks and the man that works may be broken down, in a yet wiser age, in other ways than by hostile combination." See Harper's Magazine, May, 1872,— "Saltaire and its Founder." This popular and useful magazine has rendered good service to American and English readers by its attention to industrial experiments and social questions.

here. Time which otherwise might be wasted at the rum-
shops, or spent in listless inactivity at home, is here improved
to purposes of health and recreation. Those whose constant
work is in noisy mills enjoy, I know, the green fields and the
woods greatly; and hence they resort to these grounds when-
ever they can. I heartily approved of the scheme when it
was first talked of, and thus far I know of no other than good
results from it."

A less idyllic but more generally characteristic picture of
the amusements afforded by the best New England manufacturing towns is seen in the following extracts from a letter to
the writer of this pamphlet by Mr. F. J. Kingsbury, of
Waterbury, Connecticut: " In Waterbury we have, near by
us, woods and fields which the public are free to traverse and
large tracts of open land where Irish boys play ball and build
bonfires and steal wood and corn and set the woods on fire,
and enjoy themselves much. We have a rural cemetery of
thirty acres or so neatly laid out, where people can go and
walk if they will behave themselves tolerably well, but picnics
are not allowed. We have a ball ground (admittance twenty-
five cents) well patronized, also a Y. M. C. A. ground for ball
and other games. A public square of three or four acres and
a band-stand with electric lights, but no seats. We have a
toboggan slide and several beer gardens, all for workingmen
who will pay for them. With perhaps some slight variations,
the above may be taken as a description of any of the larger
towns in the state. In my youth the workingmen and boys
had debating clubs in the winter time. I think these are not
wholly unknown among workingmen even now; but debating and discussion of questions, abstract or concrete, is much
less the fashion now, whether with the workingman or the
college student, than it was a generation ago.

" I should say that the greater portion of the amusements
of the working people is furnished now by various organizations, such as masons, odd fellows, young men's Christian
associations, fire companies, military organizations, and others

of a less general character.   Many of the churches, too, seem
to be turned into pleasure-seeking clubs.   Under these associations, excursions are made, picnics organized, games played,
dramatic exhibitions, lectures, and concerts exploited.   The
grounds for these, so far as they can be carried on in the open
air, are largely furnished by railroad companies, who have
grounds for the purpose neatly laid out and well cared for,
somewhere on the line of the track, in the vicinity of every
large town, furnished with boats, swings, bowling alleys,
tennis-courts, etc., which they allow parties free use of under
certain restrictions, getting their remuneration from the trans-
portation which results in carrying parties to and fro.   Many
of these organizations are encouraged and assisted by the
public, by contributions and in other ways, with a view, more
or less clearly defined, of furnishing healthy diversion to the
working people.   I know of no case, however, where these
have been encouraged systematically with this avowed object
in view.

" In Western Connecticut, the laborers are largely owners
of their own homes.   The care and adornment of these fur-
nishes a desirable occupation and recreation to the owners.
We have in this town whole streets of houses with neat court-
yards, with flowers both out and inside, and all the surroundings not only pleasant and cheerful but elegant.   This is to
my mind a very important factor in the well-being of our
laboring class.

" It is always dangerous to the moral stamina of a people
to do too much for them.   The impulse must come from
inside, from the people themselves, to be successful; then they
can be helped and encouraged; but, to get any good results
that will be permanent, the people themselves must wield the
laboring oar."

These sensible words by Mr. Kingsbury contain a wholesome corrective to extreme forms of social charity which would
do all and exact nothing.   Mr. Kingsbury points out, more-
over, the healthy growth now actually apparent amid the envi-

ronment of New England workingmen, and also the evils and abuses with which all local reformers are compelled to struggle.

### SUMMER GARDENS.

Philanthropists and city fathers have very one-sided ideas concerning the requirements of public parks. What men, women, and children need, in our large towns, is not simply a magnificent rural estate, a vast domain, several miles from where they live, costing time and money to visit; they want also summer-gardens near home, bits of open ground and green grass here and there throughout the vast Sahara of brick houses, paved streets, and sidewalks. Every great city needs air-holes. There ought to be a general law requiring a certain per cent. of all land laid out for building purposes in towns to be kept open, like thoroughfares for the public. Most American cities have unconsciously or wilfully drifted away from the wholesome example of old English municipal life, with its town commons and numerous open spaces. New York is one of the first to attempt to recover its lost ground. Mayor Hewitt has taken the lead in securing breathing spaces for the densely-populated districts of the great metropolis. An act has recently passed the New York legislature to provide for the location, acquisition, construction, and improvement of additional parks in the city of New York and this act was signed by Governor Hill May 14, 1887, the same day as that on which the People's Palace was opened in London. The board of street opening and improvement have power to condemn property and open as many parks below 155th Street as they may think best. It is a colossal power to grant to a municipal board but the public health requires it.

Upon the subject of the sanitary, physical, and educational advantages of Interior Open Spaces in Large Cities there was a valuable paper read before the American Public Health Association, in 1882, and now published, by Timothy-Newell, M. D., of Providence, R. I., author of a pamphlet of the Parks

of the leading cities of this country and their advantages, with
special consideration of the Parks of Providence.   On the
Justifying Value of a Public Park, there is a good paper by
Frederick Law Olmsted, a specialist in such matters, published
in the Journal of American Social Science, No. 12.   The
Nineteenth Century for May, 1887, has an article on Breathing
Spaces for Cities.   Brabazon's Social Arrows contains one or
two good articles entitled a "Plea for Public Playgrounds."
The Social Statistics of American Cities, tenth census, contain
a full account of the parks and pleasure-grounds, as well as
the means of popular amusements in our large towns.

## JEVONS ON AMUSEMENTS.

A very suggestive essay upon the subject of Amusements
for the People is that by W. Stanley Jevons, first published in
the *Contemporary Review* for October, 1878, and since made
the initial chapter of his book on Methods of Social Reform
(1883).   Professor Jevons points out the degradation into
which the sports and fairs of " Merrie England " have fallen.
He draws a striking contrast between the brutality of popular
amusements in his own country and the elevating healthful
recreations of the Continent.   He recognizes, however, the good
which the Crystal Palace has done in England and says it is
" the most admirable institution in the country. . . .   It has
proved, once for all, that with noble surroundings, with beautiful objects of attraction, and with abundance of good music,
the largest masses of people may recreate themselves, even in
the neighborhood of London, with propriety and freedom from
moral harm."   He quotes authority for the statement that
" not one person in a million among the visitors to the Crystal
Palace is charged with drunken and disorderly conduct," and
says "this is worth a volume in itself."   Mr. Jevons unhesi-
tatingly asserts that the deliberate cultivation of public amusement is the principal means toward a higher civilization.
He advocates especially the cultivation of music and restful

3

open-air concerts, where people sit tranquilly and enjoy the
highest of the arts. Mr. Jevons agrees with Aristotle (Politics, book viii.) that music is the best means of recreation.
The great superiority of the Danish common people in Copenhagen to the English in London, as regards good breeding
and general culture, Mr. Jevons attributes not alone to popular
education but to the Tivoli Gardens and the Thorwaldsen
Museum. The history and degeneration of open-air places of
amusement in England is suggested by Jevons upon the authority of Knight's Pictorial History, Morley's Bartholomew
Fair, and Stowe's Survey of London.

In another essay, the Use and Abuse of Museums, now
first published in the posthumous volume above mentioned,
Professor Jevons criticises the present arrangement and administration of museums. "There seems to be a prevalent
idea that if the populace can only be got to walk about a great
building filled with tall glass-cases, full of beautiful objects,
especially when illuminated by the electric light, they will
become civilized." Mr. Jevons thinks the multiplicity of
objects is too distracting and advocates a greater unity of effect
by better classification and local distribution. For example,
he would endeavor to differentiate and bring out clearly and
sharply the characteristics of Greek life and art, without con-
fusing and jostling it with Assyrian or Egyptian art. He
would concentrate attention upon particular things, as upon
the Pompeian House at the Crystal Palace, where the beholder
has a perfect picture of Roman life and manners. Mr. Jevons
thinks the great charm and wonderful influence of the Thorwaldsen Museum at Copenhagen are due to the unity of im-
pression made by the works of one great artist upon the
popular mind. Thus would Mr. Jevons have all museum
collections grouped and sharply distinguished by effective
contrasts. He would introduce the museum-idea into our
public schools, but would not exhibit too much at a time.
He would have things kept in a cupboard or under opaque
glass and brought out, a few at a time, like illustrative dia-

grams, to serve a particular purpose of instruction. There is great sense in all this and at the same time great encouragement to small exhibitions and small collectors. It is safe to say that, in every community, the public can be really more profited by having their attention directed to a few good pictures or a few choice things worth seeing in sequence and by a well-arranged succession of special exhibitions, artistic or industrial, than by bewildering the mind with a chaos of impressions, like that produced by one day in the British or South Kensington Museum. Mr. Jevons intimates that the attentive study of a steam-mill grinding coffee in a shop-window will do a boy more good than a run through the galleries of England's greatest collections of art and nature. He says " The whole British Museum will not teach a youth as much as he will learn by collecting a few fossils or a few minerals, *in situ* if possible, and taking them home to examine and read about.

### BESANT ON AMUSEMENTS.

Walter Besant, the English novelist, is the author of an excellent article on the Amusements of the People, in the *Contemporary Review* for March, 1884. He shows that, within a century, England has outgrown the ruder amusements of bull- and bear-baiting, dog-fights, cock-fights, rat-fights, prize-fights, " open air floggings for the joy of the people," etc. The workingmen of our time have learned to read; but the facilities for reading are still wofully inadequate, *e. g.*, " one free library for every half-million " of people in London. The present amusements of working people are theatres, music halls, public houses, Sunday excursions, and the parks. The great mass of men have no accomplishments and no healthful games. They are not taught to enjoy life. " The Bethnal Green Museum does no more to educate the people than the British Museum." Mr. Besant pictures a People's Palace, where there shall be class-rooms for all kinds of study; concert-rooms; conversation-rooms; a gymnasium; a library; and a winter garden. The practical arts as well as literature and science should be taught. By the ladder of learning men should mount unto higher things, "as has ever been the goodly and godly custom in this realm of England."

Mr. Besant pays a warm tribute to the work of Mr. Charles Leland in Philadelphia who has quietly instituted an academy of the minor arts, for teaching "shop-girls, work-girls, factory-girls, boys and young men of all classes together," certain useful and ornamental arts. "What has been done in Philadelphia amounts, in fact, to this; that one man who loves his brother man is bringing purpose, brightness, and hope into thousands of lives previously made dismal by hard and monotonous work." The same kind of work is in progress in the Maryland Institute of Baltimore, although among people of a higher class. In the *Contemporary Review* for February, 1887, Mr. Besant has described in greater detail the People's Palace which is now a reality in London. The subject of Amusements for the Poor in this country was treated some years ago in a magazine article published in the *Old and New* (now discontinued) Vol. X, p. 258. The Recreation of the People is the subject of a paper in the *Journal of American Social Science*, No. 12, by George B. Bartlett.

## THE HOUSING OF LABOR.

The establishment of more healthful conditions of home-life for the laboring class is another problem worthy of careful study and organized philanthropy. George Peabody, of Baltimore and London, set the world a lasting example in the institution of improved tenement-houses for the poor of London. The Homes of the London Poor have been described by Octavia Hill, who has "thrown much light on the problem of preventing pauperism by improving the homes of the poor." The Housing of the London Poor is treated also in the *Contemporary Review* for February, 1884. There is considerable literature upon the general subject. Mr. R. R. Bowker is

the author of a valuable article on Workingmen's Homes,
which appeared in *Harper's Monthly Magazine*, for April,
1884. In *Scribner's Magazine* for February, 1876, is an
article by Charles Barnard on A Hundred Thousand Homes,
"descriptive of the small houses of Philadelphia and the
system by which poor people became their owners." A Building System for great Cities is described in the *Penn Monthly*
for April, 1877, by Hon. Lorin Blodget. The Tenement
House System of New York, with facts and statistics, is the
subject of a pamphlet report by H. E. Pellew, New York,
1879. Improved Dwellings for the Laboring Classes is the
title of papers by Alfred T. White, who treats his theme from
a business point of view. In 1885, a royal commission published its first report on the Housing of the Working Classes
in England and Wales. "How the Poor live," by G. R.
Sims, presents a sad picture of the condition of London's poor.
It is estimated that there are forty thousand families in that
city occupying each not more than a single room. A quarter
of a million of English people living like pigs in a sty ! Professor Huxley declares that the condition of society in these
"slums" is worse than that of West African savages. A
writer in the *Contemporary Review* for February, 1884, on the
Housing of the London Poor, says : "Family life with one
room to a family—a sole chamber in which to be born, to eat,
to drink, to sleep, to work, to live, to be ill, to die, and to be
laid out in after death, is not the ideal dwelling either of
the sanitary or of the social reformer." The most distressing
moral picture of domestic communism in these slums is given
in a tract called The Bitter Cry of Outcast London. This
one tract has done much to awaken charitable England to the
horrors of the London situation. Lazarus at the Gate, by
Francis Peek, author of Social Wreckage, is a stirring appeal
for legislation which shall reach landlords who allow such
horrors as now prevail in their tenement-houses (see *Contemporary Review* for January, 1884).

Die Stätten des Elends in London, is the subject of an

article in the *Deutsche Rundschau* for January, 1885, by
Albert Duncker.   Professor Huber is the author of a monograph upon *Wohnungsnoth der kleinen Leute in grossen Städten.*
A very practical and detailed work on buildings for workingmen has been published in Prussia with the title *Die
Einrichtungen für die Wohlfahrt der Arbeiter der grösseren
gewerblichen Anlagen im Preussischen Staate,* with a book of
plates, showing plans of construction, pictures of houses, etc.
The work was published under the direction of the ministry
of commerce, industry, and public works, Berlin, 1876.   More
accessible to American readers and of immense practical value
is Carroll D. Wright's report on the Factory System of the
United States, with pictures of model houses for workingmen
in England, France, Belgium, Prussia, Connecticut, and Massachusetts (United States Census, 1880, Statistics of Manufactures).
The Social Statistics of Cities, also published in the Tenth
Census, compiled by George E. Waring, Jr., is an invaluable work and a great honor to statistical and sociological
science in America.   In this connection these statistics are
valuable for the study of questions of house-drainage and
sanitation.   The work contains also the history of American
towns and cities, with an account of their institutions, and with
instructive municipal maps.

## SAVINGS BANKS.

The promotion of economy and savings among the working
classes is one of the highest kinds of organized charity.   It
promotes thrift and self-respect.   "A History of the Banks
of Saving in Great Britain," by William Lewins, London,
1866, is by far the best work in English.   It is a masterly
account not only of the actual operations of English Savings
Banks with their beneficent effect upon the poorer classes,
but it traces the course of all philanthropic efforts that have
made progress in this field.   Lewins' description of the origin
and establishment of the Postal Savings Banks is especially
good.

Professor Laurent of Ghent, is the father of School Savings Banks and has published valuable pamphlets on the subject. England, France and Germany, got their cue for their School Savings Banks from the system established by him in Belgium.

*Le Journal des Économistes* and *L'Économiste Français* contains many good articles on the French System.

The German *Jahrbücher für Nationalökonomie und Statistik und für Gesetzgebung,* and the *Vierteljahrschrift für Volkswirthschaft* all contain discussions of the German Municipal Savings Banks and the proposed Postal system.

The best international statistics of savings are those published by the Bureau of Royal Statistics of Italy.

The "History of Savings Banks in the United States," 2 vols., 1878, by Emerson W. Keyes, includes in a well-arranged and compact form all the important facts bearing upon the growth and reverses of these institutions in America from their inception in 1816 down to 1877. Mr. Keyes singles out in an admirable way the test provisions in the laws pertaining to savings banks, such as those regulating the investment of their funds and their supervision. But the banks are treated too much as an end in themselves.

The *Bankers Magazine* contains summaries of reports as they appeared, and now and then it has articles discussing the different systems of savings.

The state reports of the savings banks in the New England and Middle States are valuable to the student.

## POOR LAWS AND PAUPERISM IN ENGLAND.

The condition of English and American almshouses and workhouses, and other agencies for the relief of pauperism cannot be understood without some historical reading. The poor laws of this country are based upon those of England, and the latter proceed from a remarkable statute of the forty-third year of Queen Elizabeth (cap. ii.), 1601, an Act for the Relief of the Poor. Three principles are embodied in this law : (1) the provision "for setting to work all such persons married or unmarried having no means to maintain them and use no ordinary and daily trade of life to get their living by;" (2) Relief of the lame, impotent, old, blind, and such other among them being poor or unable to work; and (3) Putting out of neglected children to be apprentices. Of this statute, Sir George Nicholls, in his History of the English Poor Law, says: "the great turning-point of our Poor Law Legislation is still the foundation and text-book of English Poor Law." The circumstances which led to this enactment, and the subsequent legislation, especially that which proceeds from the inquiries of the poor-law commissions (1830-37) may be fully understood by a perusal of Nicholl's work. He is also author of a History of the Scotch and Irish Poor Laws. In the English Citizen Series a volume by the Rev. T. W. Fowle is devoted to the Poor Law (London, 1881).

The report of the Poor-Law Commission, published in 1834, has great historical value and was reprinted not long ago by government-order. The Poor Law of Foreign Countries is the subject of a special report by the Local Government Board, 1875. F. C. Montague, in a Cobden-Club tract, on the Old Poor Law and New Socialism, reviews the operation of English Poor Laws and strongly opposes state-charity. In reading this tract, one is impressed with the fact that England has repeated, in a modified form, the old Roman experiment of largesses to the common people, which inevitably result in pauperism. The principles of legislation with regard to property given for charitable and other public uses is the subject of a valuable work by Courtney Stanhope Kenny, published in London in 1880. Francis Peek is the author of Social Wreckage, a review of the laws of England as they affect the Poor. A. W. Sieveking has treated the principles of charitable work. Pauperism and Self Help is the subject of an article in the Westminster Review, 103 : 107. Octavia Hill has written on the Importance of aiding the Poor without Almsgiving. Florence Hill has called attention to the Children of the State and the training of Juvenile Paupers.  *Das Englische Armenwesen* is treated in the German *Jahrbuch für Gesetzgebung,* 1886, p. 199.  London Alms and London Pauperism is the subject of an article in the *London Quarterly,* for October, 1876.  Pauperization, its Cause and Cure, and Depauperization are two tracts by Sir Baldwin Leighton. Thrift as a test of Out-door Relief is a pamphlet by George Bartlett.

### PAUPERISM AND CHARITIES ON THE CONTINENT OF EUROPE.

While the experience of England in the improvement of the condition of society is most available for Americans, it is important to add that France, Germany, and indeed all Europe have a vast fund of practical lessons which may be drawn upon by the use of special literature.  For example the charities of Paris are described by Jules Lecomte in his work entitled *La Charité à Paris,* 1861.  A great variety of educational, charitable, and other experiments are described by John De Liefde in his "Six Months among the Charities of Europe" (Alexander Strahan, London and New York, 1866). In two octavo volumes the author has recorded not only his personal observations but a digest of a vast quantity of official reports and administrative facts.  The work is not so valuable from the standpoint of organized charities as it is for its detailed description of individual charities, particularly in the education of poor or neglected children.  The writer gives the history and results of many interesting sociological experiments in France, Switzerland, Germany, and Holland.  The Poor-law System of Elberfeld has been described in a report by Andrew Doyle, London, 1871, and by the Rev. W. W. Edwards in the *Contemporary Review,* for July, 1878, and in *Good Words,* i, 5.  Mr. Sanford of the Johns Hopkins University has prepared a paper upon the same subject.  Poor Relief in different Parts of Europe is the subject of a selection of essays from the

German, by A. Emminghaus, London, 1873. Roper's translation of Grellman's work on Beggars, a work written in 1787,
affords a remarkable glimpse into beggar-life. Tramps are
not a modern institution. They are a sturdy stock, of mediæval ancestry, as prolific as fleas and even harder to kill. Upon
the sturdy beggar class two excellent works have been published in London since 1880 : (1) London and Mendicant Wan-
derers in the Streets of London, and (2) Beggar Biographies.

The subject of Pauperism in Europe has been well treated
by our countryman, Mr. Charles L. Brace, in the *North
American Review*, 120 : 315. Pauperism in France is the
subject of papers in the *Foreign Quarterly Review*, 15 : 159,
and in the *Westminster Review*, 57 : 239. Charities in France
have been characterized in *The Nation*, 4 : 270. A general
and standard treatise on Charity is that by J. M. Gérando,
De la Bienfaisance Publique, four volumes, Paris, 1839. Die
Erhebung der niederen Volksclassen is a valuable German
monograph of 168 pages. Die Verhandlungen des Deutschen
Vereins für Armenflege are standard sources of information
upon German charities. A valuable chapter upon the Poor
of Germany, Das Armenwesen, may be found in Schönberg's
encyclopædic work on Political Economy.

A French writer, De Villeneuve-Bargemont, has treated
the subject of Économie Politique Chrétienne, ou Recherches
sur la Nature et les Causes du Paupérisme en Europe et sur
les Moyens de le soulager et de le prévenir, 3 vols., Paris,
1834. Uhlhorn has treated the subject of Christian Charity
in the early church.

## Social Studies in Europe.

Among the most valuable studies of social phenomena upon
the continent of Europe are W. H. Riehl's *Land und Leute*
and Frederick Le Play's *Les Ouvriers Européens*. Both of
these writers travelled on foot through the countries and social
scenes which they describe. Le Play's studies of the actual

condition of the laboring classes in factories and in the mines are especially valuable.    He gathered illustrative facts upon a large scale and made social science concrete instead of doctrinaire, as it had been in Paris before his time.    Through the force of his example, there was founded, at the suggestion of the French Academy, an international society for practical studies in social economy, which has already published five or six volumes of monographs with the general title *Les Ouvriers des Deux Mondes*.    Le Play's ideas have penetrated all France and have led to the establishment of local unions for the study of social and economic questions.    The International society and the local *Unions de la Paix Sociale* are represented in periodical literature by *La Réforme Sociale* and by *La Science Sociale*.    A good account of this interesting movement, which is surely settling the labor question in France, may be found in the *Popular Science Monthly*, for October, 1886, Le Play's Studies in Social Phenomena, by Mr. A. G. Warner, of the Charity Organization Society of Baltimore.

## HISTORICAL RETROSPECT.

The Literature of Charities may be approached from various points of view, but best of all, in the writer's judgment is the historical.    If one would really understand the movements of social science and organized charities in the nineteenth century, he should at the outset grasp the fundamental fact that, for eighteen centuries, the charitable and legislative efforts of society have been pauperizing instead of elevating men. The process of degradation began in Italy, under the Roman empire, in the free distribution of bread and wine to the Roman populace or proletariat.    Free corn and free drink served the same purpose as our modern soup-houses and barbecues.    They made paupers and secured votes.    If you wish to study the full significance of this bottom fact which endures in the pauperism of Rome and Naples, study the history of the Roman empire, in any of the standard authorities.

The Christian Church took up the charitable work of the Roman Empire, in a different spirit indeed and with many noble results; but *some* of the methods of Christian deacons and pious monks were as radically wrong as those of the Cæsars. Miscellaneous almsgiving, bequests to the poor, and the prodigal distribution of food from wealthy monasteries, which had no other use for the surplus produce of their lands except to give it away, completed that wretched process of pauperizing the fairest, richest country in Europe. The horrid sights which greet every traveller in Italy, along the roadsides and bridges, in the public squares and at the very doors of Christian churches, are only too familiar. Men and women deliberately make themselves hideous beggars. They cripple their own children in order to work on public sympathy. I was told by one of my students, who has lived many years in Rome, that he once caught a degenerate Roman citizen transforming himself into an artificial leper by the skilful application of candle-grease and tobacco-juice to his neck and arms.

For eighteen centuries Christian charity, often given at the entrance of church-doors, has been producing professional beggars and systematic frauds. If you do not believe it, use your own eyes when you go to Italy, and then study the history of the Church and its Monasteries from an economic point of view, in Gibbon, Milman, and Villeneuve-Bargemont. Do not understand me as underrating the good works of either the church or monastery. I am speaking only of their mistaken methods of exercising charity. All that is best in our modern civilization, our schools and universities, our science and our religion, our literature and our art, have developed from the mediæval church and the old Græco-Roman empire; but in the great work of organizing charity into self-help, the nineteenth century has surely made some progress beyond the wasteful and pauperizing methods of previous ages.

# APPENDIX.

## ENGLISH CHARITY ORGANIZATIONS.

### By D. R. RANDALL, PH. D.

(Reprinted from the *Baltimore Sun*, March 30, 1887.)

Though Baltimore began the work of organizing her charities after certain other American cities, yet she had the wisdom and the opportunity to go to original sources for her information regarding the work. When Judge Fisher, of this city, was in London, he made an examination of the practical operations of the society there, and was able to help in the work already under way in Baltimore by the employment of the information so acquired. Thus, as we turn from the work in America to that in Europe, it is natural to begin with England.

The task of bringing order out of the chaotic mass of English charities has been going on during most of the present century, and the final efforts at systematizing benevolence have been helped to their present very successful issue by such men as Gladstone, Ruskin, and Cardinal Newman. Americans have been slow to recognize the fact that in this country poverty can really exist as an institution. But when we can no longer shun the conclusion that not only the poor but the paupers are with us to stay, there is manifest wisdom in seeking what may be found to have value for us in the experience of the older countries. England's experience in dealing with the poor has ranged all the way from the enactment of laws that paid men to be idle and put a premium on illegitimate children to a system of charity organization that so unifies and directs the forces of public and private charity as to afford a working model for most of the countries of the world.

An integral part of the great mass of English charities has always been the poor-law system of relief, a compulsory alms levied by the State upon landowners. The system was begun during the last years of Elizabeth's reign, with the prominent idea of supplying in-door work-house aid to the destitute poor. The administrative abuse of this system and its prostitution to political ends had produced at the beginning of this century a most deplorable condition of affairs among the poor. Out-door relief, without

45

inquiry or examination concerning its necessity or final disposition, had become universal, and nearly eight millions sterling were annually spent in this grand scheme of pauperizing. Two thousand justices, fifteen thousand vestries, and fifteen thousand sets of overseers, acting independently, doled out this national fund, yearly rendering its recipients more dependent and degraded. In 1834 the poor law was amended, and the resultant law still remains in force. Even with this amended law, as usually administered, the idea of the new charity movement has been in constant conflict, but wherever the poor authorities have consented to co-operate with the charity organizations of the various cities, much has been accomplished to increase the effectiveness of each and to better the condition of the poor.

Encouraged by the Society of Friends, William Allen and Elizabeth Fry, in the early part of this century, took up the struggle for better methods of dealing with the pauper and criminal classes. Their work among the convicts of Newgate, their attempts to relieve by national legislation the distress bequeathed the English people by wars with Napoleon, and their organization of societies for the systematic visiting of the poor, were the first effectual efforts towards the development of the later and more ideal charity.

In 1832 Dr. Chalmers, of Glasgow, arraigned the poor-law system with its compulsory provision for the poor, and declared the effect of it to be that "by a sort of festering and spreading operation the sphere of destitution is constantly widening in every parish where the benevolence of love has been superseded by the benevolence of law."

Chalmers was willing to practice that he preached, and thought the government system of relief so bad that for his own parish of St. John's he refused the assistance that the poor-law authorities offered, and dividing his parish of ten thousand inhabitants into districts, he organized the people for individual work. They visited among the poor, trying to encourage the inclination to self-help, and when immediate aid was necessary, drawing upon the small voluntary alms-fund of the parish. The good effects of these methods, as compared with the unsystematic wholesale distribution of alms by the public authorities, were so apparent that it was adopted throughout the city of Glasgow. The Chalmers system stands for the introduction of a sympathetic personal element into charity, in contradistinction to the soulless help of the State, given out by means of administrative machinery.

Octavia Hill began in 1864 the work of reforming the London tenement-houses, her work resembling Chalmers's, in that it included personal acquaintance with the poor. John Ruskin helped her to begin with a loan of £1,000, and to Baltimoreans it is of interest to remember that George Peabody left a large sum for the advancement of her work. She is at present the centre of a planetary system of workers who have the care of three thousand tenants in the city of London. The Peabody Fund alone had, in 1883, been the means of constructing upon ground cleared of loathsome shanties 3,553 suitable dwellings, occupied by 14,604 persons. The best feature of this work is that once begun it pays its own way. The rents are collected by ladies, who are personal friends of the tenants; but they are collected none the less promptly, and instead of subsidizing laziness and impotence, the interest on the original bequest can be used to extend the work.

With such examples to learn from, and with the experience of that universal society, St. Vincent de Paul, to guide them, men like Cardinal Newman and William E. Gladstone took hold of the work of building up the London Charity Organization Society. That society stands to-day as the greatest co-operative work of the character undertaken, and has furnished an incentive and a model for cities in England, France, Germany, and our own country. The promoters of the plan aimed at nothing less than bringing all the charities of London, whether State, corporate or individual, into correspondence and concert of administration. Their own organization was to be the means through which this concerted action was to be achieved without violation of chartered rights or interference with individual methods.

In London everything is on a gigantic scale and the needs of the poor are no exception to the rule. The number of paupers relieved in London on one day of the third week in last February was over 105,000. From the country districts, the idle, the dissolute, the despairing, all flock to the metropolis and further aggravate the evils of overpopulation. Acres upon acres of huts, court-yards and alleys, the resorts of none but the criminal classes, the haunts of evil and most loathsome squalor, the outcome of ignorance, idleness and vice, where all purity is stifled in infancy—these are the fields of the society's work. Whole classes in London eat their bread on the condition not merely of good conduct but of favorable seasons. A three-days' rain will reduce thirty thousand "costermongers" or venders of provisions to the very verge of starvation.

To alleviate in one way or another the suffering entailed by this great mass of misfortune and vice, over nine hundred charitable foundations existed in London alone, and in that single city five millions sterling were annually distributed by private munificence, and all this in addition to the "poor rates," the proceeds of which were distributed by public officials. The Charity Organization addressed itself to the great task of systematizing this vast number of incongruous charities, and did not shrink from setting forth an ideal as high as that contained in this extract from the enumeration of the general objects of the society: " By its system, when perfected, it is expected that no loop-hole will be left for imposture; no dark holes and corners of misery, disease and corruption remain unvisited ; no social sores fester untouched by wise and gentle hands; no barriers of ignorance or selfish apathy stand unassailed between the rich and the poor; no differences of creed prevent unity of action in the common cause of humanity."

The influence of intelligence and care in the disposition of private alms as well as of State-help has worked the greatest moral as well as economic good. Members of the boards of guardians of the poor are now among the leaders in the new charity movement. The clergy of all denominations and the State and city officials co-operate with heart and mind. Trustees of charitable bequests and institutions are gradually realizing that true charity does not consist in sitting in one's office beside a heap of shillings and filling each unfortunate hand that is thrust in sight. Co-operation is certainly the law of the new and coming charity, even though many fail to believe in its applicability in the industrial world. Co-operation prevents "overlapping" of relief, which independent action renders almost inevitable, while the careful investigation stops imposition by making it possible to discriminate between real and merely alleged destitution.

The results of this movement have been most marked in London, because there the experience acquired has been greatest, the centralization of the work is more complete, and the relations with the poor authorities are more intimate. Since the beginning of the work, in 1869, the poor rate has fallen 30 per cent. The decreasing expenditures of the various charitable organizations, the decreasing number of mendicants, and the arrest of many in their downward course towards pauperism attest the value of the results attained. In six of the Poor Unions of London in ten years the number of paupers decreased 12,108, or from 26,289 at the beginning of the decade to 14,181 at the end; while in the same district the attendence upon the public schools nearly trebled. In the Farmain Union, comprising some of the southern counties, the number of paupers was reduced from 49,332 in 1876 to 39,117 in 1886, while during the same period the expenses for help of the poor decreased from £261,000 to £194,841.

Such results are the outcome of the substitution of in-door relief after investigation of each case for the old, wholesale, indiscriminate plan. A system of organized charity which has been administered with such success in London, with its great population, its conflicting interests, and institutional conservatism, ought to be and can be maintained in Baltimore, for this city has not only the warm hearts and long purses that place great sums at the disposal of the needy, but it has the will and the intelligence to turn the power of this wise benevolence in the direction of constructive, helpful charity.

www.ingramcontent.com/pod-product-compliance
Lightning Source LLC
Chambersburg PA
CBHW030724110426
42739CB00030B/1363